A Beginning-to-Read Book

In the Woods

by Mary Lindeen

NORWOOD HOUSE PRESS

DEAR CAREGIVER, The *Beginning to Read—Read and Discover* books provide emergent readers the opportunity to explore the world through nonfiction while building early reading skills. The text integrates both common sight words and content vocabulary. These key words are featured on lists provided at the back of the book to help your child expand his or her sight word recognition, which helps build reading fluency. The content words expand vocabulary and support comprehension.

Nonfiction text is any text that is factual. The Common Core State Standards call for an increase in the amount of informational text reading among students. The Standards aim to promote college and career readiness among students. Preparation for college and career endeavors requires proficiency in reading complex informational texts in a variety of content areas. You can help your child build a foundation by introducing nonfiction early. To further support the CCSS, you will find Reading Reinforcement activities at the back of the book that are aligned to these Standards.

Above all, the most important part of the reading experience is to have fun and enjoy it!

Sincerely,

Shannon Cannon

Shannon Cannon, Ph.D.
Literacy Consultant

Norwood House Press • P.O. Box 316598 • Chicago, Illinois 60631
For more information about Norwood House Press please visit our website at
www.norwoodhousepress.com or call 866-565-2900.
© 2016 Norwood House Press. Beginning-to-Read™ is a trademark of Norwood House Press.
All rights reserved. No part of this book may be reproduced or utilized in any form or by any
means without written permission from the publisher.

Editor: Judy Kentor Schmauss
Designer: Lindaanne Donohoe

Photo Credits:

Shutterstock, cover, 1, 8-9, 10-11, 12, 14-15, 18-19, 20-21, 22-23, 24-25, 26, 27, 28-29;
Phil Martin, 3, 4-5, 6-7, 13, 16-17

Library of Congress Cataloging-in-Publication Data
    Lindeen, Mary.
    In the woods / by Mary Lindeen.
        pages cm. – (A beginning to read book)
    Summary: "Take a walk in the woods. You can see trees, birds, squirrels, deer, and flowers.
There are many interesting plants and animals that live in the woods. See what you can find!
This title includes reading activities and a word list"– Provided by publisher.
    Audience: Grades K to grade 3.
    ISBN 978-1-59953-697-2 (library edition : alk. paper)
    ISBN 978-1-60357-782-3 (ebook)
    1. Forest animals–Juvenile literature. 2. Forest plants–Juvenile
literature. I. Title.
    QH86.L567 2015
    578.73–dc23
                                                    2015001224

Manufactured in the United States of America in Stevens Point, Wisconsin. 275N–062015

We can go down this path.
Where do you think it might go?

It goes through the woods.

Woods have lots of trees and animals.

Some trees are little.

This one only has a few leaves.

Some trees are big.

This one is very big.

It goes up and up and up!

Birds live in this tree.

What do you see in this nest?

A squirrel lives in another tree.

Look at its big tail.

Look at this owl
up in the tree.

It is sleeping.

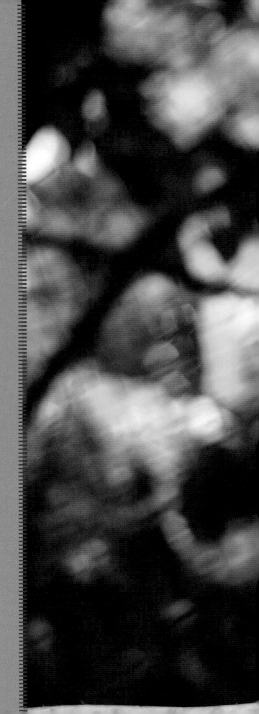

Deer live in the
woods, too.

How many do
you see?

Flowers grow in the woods.

They grow under the trees.

You can blow on this flower.

Where will the seeds go?

What is in the grass?

It is a rabbit.

It lives in the woods, too.

An old log is on the ground.

Moss grows on it.

Bugs live under it.

Here is a big stick.
It fell off of a tree.

You can use it to help you walk.

You can find so many things in the woods!

...READING REINFORCEMENT...

CRAFT AND STRUCTURE

To check your child's understanding of this book, recreate the following diagram on a sheet of paper. Read the book with your child, then help him or her fill in the diagram using what they learned. Work together to complete the diagram by writing words or ideas about the woods in the empty circles:

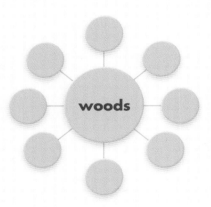

woods

VOCABULARY: Learning Content Words

Content words are words that are specific to a particular topic. All of the content words for this book can be found on page 32. Use some or all of these content words to complete one or more of the following activities:

- Create an idea web for the content words. Write a content word in the middle of the diagram. Help your child write related words and ideas in the outer circles.

- Ask your child to use his or her own words to define each of the content words. Have your child use each content word in a sentence.

- Say a content word. Have your child say the first word that comes to his or her mind. Discuss connections between the two words.

- Have your child find and cut out two magazine pictures that remind him or her of the meaning of each content word.

- Have your child think of synonyms (words with similar meanings) or antonyms (words with opposite meanings) for as many content words as possible.

FOUNDATIONAL SKILLS: Vowel digraphs *ee, ea*

Vowel digraphs are two vowels that together make a single sound (for example, *ea* as in *dream*). Have your child supply the missing vowel digraphs for each of the words below. Then help your child find the words with vowel digraphs in this book.

l _ _ v e s   s _ _ d s   t r _ _

d _ _ r   s _ _   s l _ _ p i n g

CLOSE READING OF INFORMATIONAL TEXT

Close reading helps children comprehend text. It includes reading a text, discussing it with others, and answering questions about it. Use these questions to discuss this book with your child:

- What is a path?
- How would you use a big stick?
- Why do you think squirrels live in trees?
- What do you know about trees?
- What is your favorite thing about the woods? Why?

FLUENCY

Fluency is the ability to read accurately with speed and expression. Help your child practice fluency by using one or more of the following activities:

- Reread this book to your child at least two times while he or she uses a finger to track each word as you read it.
- Read the first sentence aloud. Then have your child reread the sentence with you. Continue until you have finished this book.
- Ask your child to read aloud the words they know on each page of this book. (Your child will learn additional words with subsequent readings.)
- Have your child practice reading this book several times to improve accuracy, rate, and expression.

••• Word List •••

In the Woods uses the 80 words listed below. *High-frequency* words are those words that are used most often in the English language. They are sometimes referred to as sight words because children need to learn to recognize them automatically when they read. *Content words* are any words specific to a particular topic. Regular practice reading these words will enhance your child's ability to read with greater fluency and comprehension.

High-Frequency Words

a	find	its	see	under
an	go	little	so	up
and	goes	look	some	use
another	has	many	the	very
are	have	might	they	we
at	help	of	things	what
big	here	off	think	where
can	how	old	this	will
do	in	on	through	you
down	is	one	to	
few	it	only	too	

Content Words

animals	flower(s)	log	rabbit	tree(s)
birds	grass	lots	seeds	walk
blow	ground	moss	sleeping	woods
bugs	grow(s)	nest	squirrel	
deer	leaves	owl	stick	
fell	live(s)	path	tail	

••• About the Author

Mary Lindeen is a writer, editor, parent, and former elementary school teacher. She has written more than 100 books for children and edited many more. She specializes in early literacy instruction and books for young readers, especially nonfiction.

••• About the Advisor

Dr. Shannon Cannon is a teacher educator in the School of Education at UC Davis, where she also earned her Ph.D. in Language, Literacy, and Culture. She serves on the clinical faculty, supervising pre-service teachers and teaching elementary methods courses in reading, effective teaching, and teacher action research.